The Basketball Dribbling Guide

by   Sidney Goldstein

author of **The Basketball Coach's Bible**

and **The Basketball Player's Bible**

GOLDEN AURA PUBLISHING

The Nitty-Gritty Basketball Series

The Basketball Dribbling Guide
by Sidney Goldstein

Published by:

GOLDEN AURA PUBLISHING

Post Office Box 41012

Philadelphia, PA 19127 U.S.A.

Library of Congress Catalog Card Number: 94-96500

Goldstein, Sidney

The Basketball Dribbling Guide / Sidney Goldstein.--1st ed.

Basketball-Coaching

ISBN 1-884357-16-4

Softcover

Cover design and illustration by Lightbourne Images

copyright ©1994

Contents

Introduction

Over many years of coaching, planning, and studying, I found ways to teach each and every skill even to the most unskilled player. This scheme of learning did not come from any book. I tried things in practice. I modified them till they worked. Even players who could not simultaneously chew bubble gum and walk learned the skills. This booklet, part of **The Nitty-Gritty Basketball Series**, is one result of this effort. I believe you can benefit from my work.

Who Can Use This Information

This booklet is the perfect tool for anybody who wants to coach, teach, and/or learn basketball:

- A parent who wants to teach his or her child
- A player who wants to understand and play the game better
- A little league or recreation league coach
- A high school or junior high school coach
- A college coach, a professional coach
- A women's or a men's coach

This booklet contains material from **The Basketball Player's Bible**. Chapter 1 gives the keys to learning the skills presented. I present the skills in lesson form. Chapter 2 gives the features of each lesson. The largest chapter, Chapter 3, presents the lessons in order. Check the **Lessons Needed Before** feature as you progress.

Besides dribbling lessons, this booklet contains many ball handling lessons. Ball handling involves handling the ball, grabbing it, and keeping it away from the defense. The 2 weaves are advanced ball handling skills which involve timing and communication. **The Basketball Player's Bible** contains these lessons and many other related ones.

Golden Aura's Nitty-Gritty Basketball Series
by Sidney Goldstein
See the description in the back of this book.

The Basketball Coach's Bible

The Basketball Player's Bible

The Basketball Shooting Guide

The Basketball Scoring Guide

The Basketball Dribbling Guide

The Basketball Defense Guide

The Basketball Pass Cut Catch Guide

Basketball Fundamentals

Planning Basketball Practice

Videos for the Guides soon available

HOW TO CONTACT THE AUTHOR

The author seeks your comments about this book. Sidney Goldstein is available for consultation and clinics with coaches and players. Contact him at:

Golden Aura Publishing
PO Box 41012
Philadelphia, PA 19127
215 438-4459

Chapter One
1

Principles of Learning

How To Use The Dribbling Guide

Start from the beginning and progress through the lessons one by one. Typically, I arrange them in order of increasing difficulty. You may want to skip some topics. However, use the **Lessons Needed Before** feature to insure that you do not omit needed techniques.

The most important as well as the most frequently skipped lessons involve techniques. If you spend the needed time on these lessons, you will improve exponentially on a daily basis. Skip them and improvement may be delayed for months and even years.

One big misconception about learning the basics is that to improve you must practice things millions of times. I've tried it and so has everybody else. It does not work well. Volume of practice does not necessarily bring about improvement; practicing properly insures improvement. The following **principles** tell you what and how to practice. A list of **Counterproductive Beliefs** follows. These often widely held ideas prevent learning because they do not work.

Principles Of Dribbling

1. Dribbling starts with proper hand and arm motion as well as body position. See Lesson 1.

2. Moving and twisting to awkward body positions are keys to dribbling. See Lessons 2-4.

3. You need to dribble with defensive contact, looking in all directions, even behind, to learn how to protect the ball. Lessons 5-6 teach this.

4. Dribbling is never an end unto itself. One offensive objective is to pass the ball up court to the open player as fast as possible. You must dribble with your head up, constantly looking to pass. All lessons require players to keep their heads up and look while dribbling. Lessons 7 involves both looking and passing while dribbling.

Counterproductive Beliefs

1. Dribbling can't be taught. You have to be a natural. This is true if you don't know how to teach dribbling. This inaccurate idea discourages coaches and players alike. Nothing could be further from the truth.

2. Dribbling between the legs and behind the back are effective methods. They may look good and be okay to practice, but they do not have much effect in games.

3. It is cool to dribble waist high or higher like many of the pros. Dribbling high is much more difficult, and, unless you are very quick it will lead to disaster. Bob Cousy dribbled with his elbows nearly straight; the ball was only inches, rather than feet, off the floor.

4. The more you dribble the better you dribble. No, dribbling correctly improves dribbling. Dribbling with the head down, standing straight up, not bothering to look around does the reverse—you learn how to and do dribble incorrectly. You need to be aware of how you practice. If you want to improve your dribbling technique stop dribbling improperly, even if it is inadvertent, like the dribbling you do while shooting the ball around. Limit your dribbling to the lessons in this book.

Chapter Two
2

Lesson Features

Table Information

At a glance this table gives an overview to aid in planning. It supplies the name and number of each lesson as well as these additional features: lessons needed before, the number of players needed, the effort level, the estimated practice times, whether you need a ball and/or a court. Practice the *no ball* or *no court* lessons for homework while watching TV or sitting down. The Player's Corner section of each lesson supplies some of the same information.

Number

The lessons are numbered in order from easiest to hardest, from most fundamental to most complicated. Typically, do them in order. Sometimes you can skip. If you do, check the **Lessons Needed Before** feature so that you do not skip essential lessons.

Name

A name related to each lesson serves as a descriptive mnemonic device (I almost forgot that). When skills are executed simultaneously, their names are directly coupled like Pivot Around Shoot or Jump Hook. Lessons with skills separately performed are named, for example, Pivot with Defense, where one player pivots on offense while the other is on defense.

Brief

In one sentence (usually) the **brief** immediately familiarizes you with the lesson by stating the action and movement involved.

Why Do This

When do you use this in a game? What is the significance of the lesson? What fundamentals do you practice? How does this lesson relate to others? The **Why Do This** section answers these questions.

Directions

These are step-by-step directions for you.

Key Points

This feature emphasizes important points in the directions so that you will not make common mistakes.

When You Are More Expert

These more expert lessons usually add another step, combine another skill, or change one variable in the previous lesson. Some lessons have as many as four expert additions.

Player's Corner and Section Tables

At a glance you can see that the **Player's Corner** lists 8 useful pieces of information about each lesson. The **Table of Lessons** in **Appendix C** and each **Section Table** contain this same information. **Xs** in the tables mean <u>yes</u>. Dashes (-) mean <u>no</u>.

• Lessons Needed Before

Do these lessons before this current one. If you don't, then you will have a problem. Often you can skip lessons without it being disastrous. Not so with the lessons listed as Lessons Needed Before.

• Additional Needs

This feature gives 4 useful pieces of information.

Ball and Court

For most lessons you need a **ball** and a **court**. However, for some either one or the other or both are not needed. These lessons can be practiced at home while watching TV or in your backyard. **Xs** in the tables mean <u>yes</u>.

Players

Most lessons are for individuals. So, the Player's Corner lists additional players needed, whereas the Tables give the total number (which is always one more than additional players).

Assist

For some lessons you need an inactive **assistant** to either act as a dummy player or more importantly to closely watch what you are doing. **Xs** in the tables mean <u>yes</u>.

• Effort or Effort Level

The effort level of a lesson involves the physical effort involved. Level 1 lessons involve technique. Do them slowly;

they often do not resemble the skill performed in a game because 2 to 5 technique lessons often comprise a skill. In situations calling for defense, the defense expends little effort.

Level 2 lessons are at the practice level. Any skill practiced at a moderate pace like shooting or pivoting is at level 2. This level is a catchall for lessons between levels 1 and 3. Defense against offense makes a moderate effort.

Level 3 lessons are at the game level. Players sprint and perform at maximum effort. Pressure is on players. Offense and defense go full speed against each other. Games are easy compared to these lessons.

• Daily Practice Time

This is a time range needed to practice this lesson. Note that many lessons have additional parts. These will take more time.

• More Expert Lessons

Each of these additions adds one or two parameters to the main lesson. Few are optional. Most need to be done after you are more expert.

FEATURES OF THE DIAGRAMS

Lines and Arrows

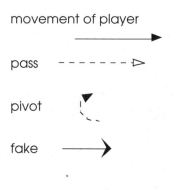

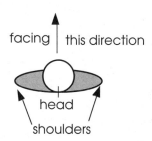

Solid lines indicate movement of players whereas dashed lines usually indicate movement of the ball. One exception is dashed lines used to show pivoting direction. The types of arrows used are solid for movement and hollow for passes. A different type of arrow head is used for fakes. See the diagrams.

Body Position of Player

The body of a player is shown from an overhead view two ways. The line or the ellipse represents the shoulders. The

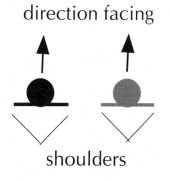

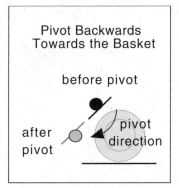

Pivot Backwards
Towards the Basket

before pivot

after pivot

pivot direction

circle shows the head. The player is always facing away from the shoulders toward the head.

Shades for Different Positions

When a player is shown in two positions in the same diagram, the first position is black and the second is lighter in color. Often offense or defense are shown in light and dark shades. In some diagrams shades are used to designate the position of a player when the ball of the same shade is in the diagramed position.

Numbers in Multistep Movements

Many drills involve multiple steps. Each step, as well, may have several timed movements that need to be executed in order. So, in the diagrams for each step, the numbers indicate the order of the movements. One (1) means first, two (2) second and so on. If two players move at the same time the numbers will be the same, so there may be several ones or twos in the diagram.

In the diagram below, there are three ones in the diagram. This indicates that these players move at the same time. There are two twos; one indicates a cut, while the other indicates a pass.

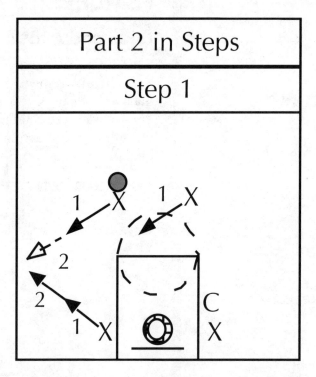

Part 2 in Steps

Step 1

Chapter Three 3 | Dribbling and Ball Handling Lessons 1-14

L E S S O N	NAME	A S S I S T	P L A Y E R S	C O U R T	B A L L	E F F O R T	L E S S O N	Lessons Before	REF TO *Coach's Manual*	DAILY TIME	E X T R A
1-14	**DRIBBLING, BALL HANDLING**										
1	Dribbling D Position	-	1	-	x	1	**1**	none	4.0	1-2	0
2	Dribble Mechanics 1-2	x	1	-	x	1-2	**2**	1	4.1	5-15	4
3	Dribble Twist	x	1	-	x	1-2	**3**	2	4.13	5-15	1
4	Follow the Leader 1-3	x	1+	-	x	1-2	**4**	3	4.2	5-15	2
5	Protect Ball	x	2	-	x	2-3	**5**	4	4.3	5-10	2
6	Dribble with D Layup	x	1+	x	x	2-3	**6**	5	4.4	10-20	0
7	Dribble Pass with D	-	3	-	x	3	**7**	5	4.5	10-20	1
8	Dribble Full Shoot	-	1	x	x	2-3	**8**	5	8.2	5-15	0
9	Driving to the Basket	-	1	x	x	2	**9**	4	8.1	5-20	2
10	Take Away	-	2	-	x	1-2	**10**	1	1.1	5-10	0
11	Move Ball	-	2	-	x	3	**11**	2	1.4	2-5	0
12	Conditioning Grab	-	2	x	x	2	**12**	10	1.2	15-30	2
13	Front Weave	-	3	x	x	2	**13**	12	9.7	10-20	0
14	Back Weave	x	3+	x	x	2	**14**	12	9.8	5-10	0

1 Dribbling D Position

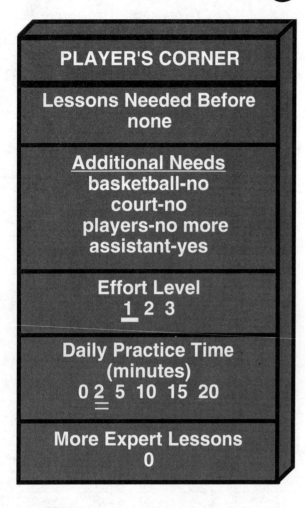

PLAYER'S CORNER

Lessons Needed Before
none

Additional Needs
basketball-no
court-no
players-no more
assistant-yes

Effort Level
<u>1</u> 2 3

Daily Practice Time
(minutes)
0 <u>2</u> 5 10 15 20

More Expert Lessons
0

Brief:
Players move their bodies and wrists in the dribbling defensive position.

Why Do This
It is no coincidence that most good dribblers are also good defensive players. The body positions for both defense and dribbling are similar. They can be practiced together. In both cases players need to be able to move in any direction as quickly as possible. The body is low to the ground with feet slightly greater than shoulder width apart. The dribbling position is more demanding than the defensive one since it entails twisting and swiveling the head, shoulders, hips, and legs in different directions. Being able to perform these twisting movements while handling the ball and looking is the key to dribbling well.

Directions
1. Start with your feet shoulder width apart. Keep the trunk straight and bend at the knees. Overdo it by bending down all the way. This is the full down position. Move half way up. This is the half down position. This is also called the ready position because you are in the best position to run.

2. Move between the full and half down positions several times.

3. In the half down position let your arms hang straight down at the sides. The back of your hands face forward, the palms face backward.

4. Flick the wrists upward and let them come back without any additional effort like we did in Lesson 2. Continue for 30 seconds.

5. Move to the full down position. Continue flicking the wrists for another 30 seconds.

6. Now move through the various positions– up,

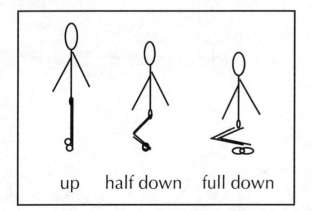

up   half down   full down

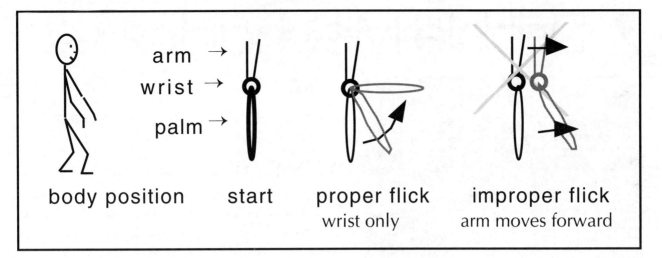

arm →
wrist →
palm →

body position   start   proper flick   improper flick
                          wrist only   arm moves forward

The Ready Position

The Unready Position

The back is bent too much and the legs too little.

half down, and full down– for another minute while continuing to flick.

Key Points

1. The wrists are loose and you flick upward only; the elbows and trunk are straight.

2. Players tend to flick the wrists forward, not up. This distinction may seem slight, but the lesson has value only if the wrists are flicked upward. The diagram shows the difference between a forward and an upward flick. In the upward flick the hand rotates nearly 90 degrees more than the forward flick.

3. The half down position is also called the ready position. Use this exclusively when on the court. Do this lesson and all extensions in the full down position to emphasize that the legs and not the trunk must be bent.

2 Dribble Mechanics 1-3

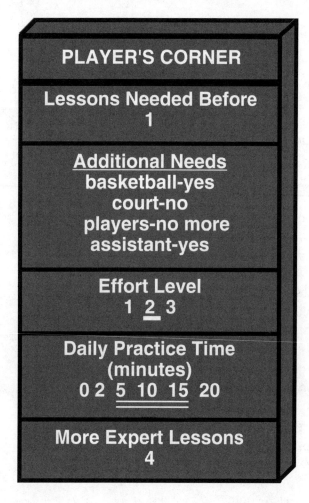

PLAYER'S CORNER

Lessons Needed Before
1

Additional Needs
basketball-yes
court-no
players-no more
assistant-yes

Effort Level
1 <u>2</u> 3

Daily Practice Time
(minutes)
0 2 <u>5 10 15</u> 20

More Expert Lessons
4

Brief:
Players dribble with each hand without and then with the ball.

Why Do This

Dribblers do two things well. One involves the movement of the hand and the wrist. The hand is clawed so that only the fingertips touch the ball; the wrist is loose; flicks of the wrist propel the ball, not arm movement. The other involves the body position. The head readily glances in any direction. The shoulders, hips, arms, legs, and other body parts are positioned to sprint as well as ward off the defense. Have an assistant give instructions visually as much as possible to insure that you keep your head up. Work in the full down position to emphasize:

1) The need to bend legs, not backs.

2) That it is easier to dribble if your hands are near the ground.

Part 1 teaches the dribbling positions without the use of the ball. This enables you to readily diagnose wrist and body position problems before the ball is used in Part 2.

Directions

Part 1

1. Start in the full down position, feet shoulder width, arms extended straight downward, elbows only slightly bent, hands straight down.

2. Mirror movements of an assistant or directly follow the directions. Continue to flick upward from each position . Each position is about 6 inches from the foot.

3. The diagram shows 9 dribbling positions; if you add corner positions the total is 13. Dribble in each position with each hand. This yields 18 positions or 26 using the corners.

4. Mirror movements rather than directly follow the assistant. When as assistant facing you uses the right hand use the left and vice-versa.

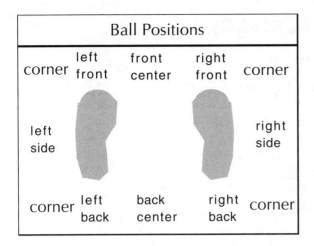

Ball Positions

corner	left front	front center	right front	corner
left side				right side
corner	left back	back center	right back	corner

Dribbling in the Full Down Position

Dribbling in the Half Down Position

5. Dribble with your right hand first. Move your hand to this position. Hold the first few positions for 10-15 seconds so that an assistant can verbally correct you. After this, hold each position for 3-8 seconds.

6. Learn the name of the positions, even though the instructions are nonverbal, so you can use this in other lessons. Here is the list: *right side, right front, front center, left front* (continue with the same hand), *left side, right back, left back, back center.* Repeat these movements with the left hand.

Part 2

7. Repeat Directions 1-6 with a ball.

8. Dribble the ball about six inches from your foot in each position. Do not turn around to dribble in back or awkward positions. Keep your head forward so you can follow the directions. Dribble in the full down position initially.

Key Points

1. The hands and palms do not touch the ball.

2. The hand is shaped like a claw. Only the fingertips touch the ball.

3. Flick the wrist to dribble; do not move the arms.

4. Dribble in the full down position.

5. In **Part 2** the ball is a maximum of 6 inches off the ground.

6. Both arms are in the same ready position for dribbling; they hang straight down at the sides with the elbows slightly bent. After more practice, move the nondribbling arm to a defensive or protective position with the elbow bent.

7. Keep your head up at all times.

8. Keep the trunk nearly vertical, not bent.

9. You need to practice dribbling with the left hand on the right side and also with the right hand on the left side.

More Expert Lessons

Continuous Dribble

More through the positions more quickly in the half down position. Keep your head up. Move the ball to every position. Hold each position for a maximum of 3 seconds. Continue for 15-60 seconds.

Tricky Movements

Try some tricky movements. Move the ball to the *center back* position and then through the legs to a *center front*. Repeat using the opposite hand. Then go from the *center front* to the *center back*. Repeat using the opposite hand.

Switch Forward Foot

Repeat the entire lesson with the left foot forward and then with the right foot forward.

Switchy Feet

Change your foot positions after doing this lesson several times. Put the left or right foot forward at any time during the lesson. Make sure your head is up and your trunk stays nearly vertical. Stay in the half down or lower position with the elbows nearly straight; the ball is 6 inches from the ground.

3 Dribble Twist

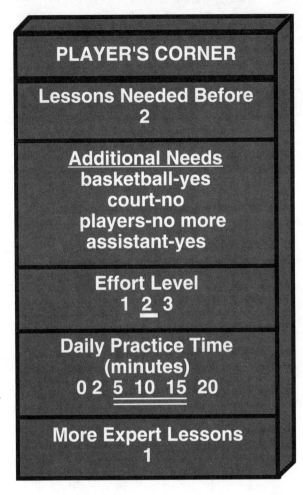

PLAYER'S CORNER

Lessons Needed Before
2

Additional Needs
basketball-yes
court-no
players-no more
assistant-yes

Effort Level
1 <u>2</u> 3

Daily Practice Time
(minutes)
0 2 <u>5</u> <u>10</u> <u>15</u> 20

More Expert Lessons
1

Brief:
Swivel the head, shoulders, and hips in every conceivable way while dribbling with each hand.

Why do this

This lesson makes an okay dribbler a very good one. You are forced to dribble in the unusual positions needed to evade the defense and protect the ball while keeping your eyes down court. You should feel like a contortionist if you are doing things correctly. It is advantageous to find an assistant to watch.

Directions

1. The directions are the same as those for lesson 2 except for the starting position. You can do this with or without the ball.

2. Move the ball in the half down (or lower) position for 15 to 60 seconds to each of the 13 ball positions. See the diagram.

3. Repeat for each of the nine body and foot positions below. See the diagram on the next page; note that three extra positions facing forward are shown.

> **a.** Face left–turn your body to the left. Swivel your shoulders forward.
>
> **b.** Face right–turn your body to the right. Swivel your shoulders forward.
>
> **c.** Face back–turn around. With some difficulty you can swivel your shoulders forward.
>
> **d.** Face left, right, and then back with the left foot forward. Three parts.
>
> **e.** Repeat **d** with the right foot forward.

4. In order to see the assistant you must rotate the head, hip, and shoulder forward. Do not swivel the feet around; they remain pointed away from the dribbling direction.

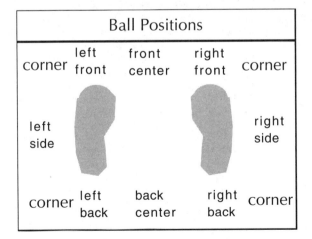

Ball Positions

corner	left front	front center	right front	corner
left side				right side
corner	left back	back center	right back	corner

Foot and Body Positions			
Head Always Faces Forward			
forward	left	right	back

right foot forward

left foot forward

5. Do this without an assistant by facing or turning to one direction each time.

6. Novices do this in the full down position first.

Key Points

1. The hands and palms do not touch the ball. The hand is shaped like a claw. Only the fingertips touch the ball. Flick the wrist to dribble; do not move the arms.

2. The ball is a maximum of 6 inches off the ground.

3. Move the nondribbling arm to a defensive or protective position with the elbow bent. Both arms are in about the same position.

4. Stay in the more than half down position.

5. The back is nearly straight.

6. The head and body swivel around to face the dribbling direction. Do not swivel the feet.

7. Novice players do this from the full down position.

8. You need to practice dribbling with the left hand on the right side and also with the right hand on the left side.

More Expert Lessons

Watch the Game

Do this while watching a game or people warming up. It is a worthwhile use of time that usually is wasted. Keep the trunk nearly vertical and the knees bent near the full down position. The ball is only inches from the ground.

4 Follow the Leader

PLAYER'S CORNER

Lessons Needed Before
3

Additional Needs
basketball-yes
court-no
players-no more
assistant-yes

Effort Level
1 <u>2</u> 3

**Daily Practice Time
(minutes)**
0 2 <u>5 10 15</u> 20

More Expert Lessons
2

X X X X X X X X X X X
Move sideways around
gym on the dotted line
using sidelines and endlines.

Brief:
Players dribble as in lessons 60 and 61 while moving.

Why Do This

This lesson is a step closer to game type dribbling. It is identical to the previous lessons with the addition of movement. The movements involve a jump step that is like a defensive sliding move.

Directions

Part 1

1. Start in the half down position with the ball on the floor out of the way. When you take a jump step to the right, do not bring your feet close together. Do not slide your feet either. If you take this step quickly, it resembles a jump to the right.

2. Take 3 jump steps to the right, then three to the left, then three forward and three back. Lead with either foot going forward and back. Repeat this several times.

3. Pick up the ball. Move in the above jump step pattern while dribbling.

4. Your assistant moves the dribbling hand to the position that you dribble. Hold positions for 2-3 seconds initially. Then increase the switching. Make sure to use each hand for equal amounts of time. Try several difficult positions as soon as possible which include:

> **a.** moving right and dribbling on the left side with the right hand;
>
> **b.** moving left while dribbling on the right side with the left hand;
>
> **c.** dribbling in the back and back center positions anytime.

5. You can do this without an assistant if you take care to move the ball around to all positions and if you keep your head up watching

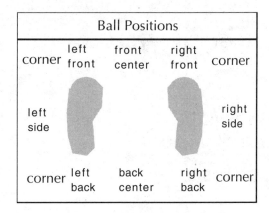

Ball Positions

corner	left front	front center	right front	corner
left side				right side
corner	left back	back center	right back	corner

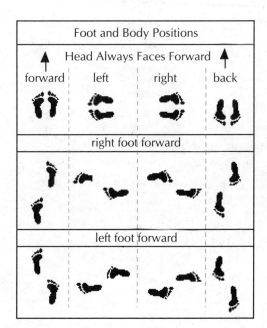

Foot and Body Positions

Head Always Faces Forward

forward	left	right	back

right foot forward

left foot forward

other players or something else. However, a good assistant can make this exercise more worthwhile as well as correct improper movement.

Part 2

6. Repeat steps 2-5 with the left foot forward and then the right foot forward.

Part 3

7. Repeat steps 2-5 facing either side or the back. In each position you must swivel at the hips and shoulders to see the assistant. This is very difficult. There are many possible positions:

> **a.** Face left.
>
> **b.** Face right.
>
> **c.** Face back.
>
> **d.** Face left, right, and then back with the left foot forward. Three parts here.
>
> **e.** Repeat **d** with the right foot forward.

Key Points

1. Move slowly at first.

2. Keep the non dribbling hand in the same position as the dribbling hand.

3. High dribbling is more difficult than low dribbling. Keep the knees bent and the elbows straight so the ball is only inches off the ground.

4. Keep the back nearly vertical.

5. Wrists flick the ball. Put lots of fingertips on the ball.

6. Jump step, do not slide.

7. This is a good workout as well.

More Expert Lessons

Twister

Pretend you have a ball. Move through a self-imagined Globe Trotter-like routine. Move in every direction, spinning around, putting the ball behind your back and through their legs. An assistant watching can easily diagnose dribbling problems. The flick of the wrist may not be strong enough. The hands may be too high off the ground. The hands may not be in the claw position for ball handling. The legs may be bent too little while the back may be bent too much.

These problems need correction before you use a ball. Even though this lesson seems strange (like many others), it is very beneficial. Doing is believing.

Twister with Ball

Do the twister routine with the ball just like you did without the ball. An assistant can flash fingers every few seconds to make sure you are looking up. Call out the numbers as you dribble.

5 Protect the Ball

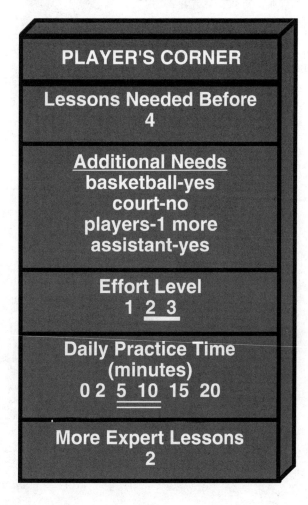

PLAYER'S CORNER

Lessons Needed Before
4

Additional Needs
basketball-yes
court-no
players-1 more
assistant-yes

Effort Level
1 <u>2</u> 3

**Daily Practice Time
(minutes)**
0 2 <u>5 10</u> 15 20

More Expert Lessons
2

Brief:
The dribbler protects the ball from an aggressive defensive player.

Why Do This

This lesson forces you to protect the ball while dribbling. An aggressive defense goes after the ball with more than normal abandon, staying in body contact with the dribbler. The dribbler is allowed to turn and swivel in a particular area, but cannot run away. The body, especially the arms, ward off the defense. Both the dribbler and defense overdo it. Technically, both constantly foul each other at first. However, players must dribble with much contact initially in order to learn. Because the defense works at maximum effort this is also a hustle lesson.

Directions

1. The defense goes aggressively after the ball of the dribbler for about 20 seconds; count out loud.

2. It is okay for the defense to make body contact; no flailing of the arms is allowed. Knocking over players is also not allowed. When the offense turns, do not stay behind facing their back. Hustle after the ball.

3. The dribbler continuously dribbles, staying in a small area. Running away from the defense defeats the purpose of the lesson. Turn and swivel one way or the other. Switch dribbling hands after 10 seconds.

4. Hold your nondribbling arm in a similar position as the dribbling arm. It is okay initially to fend off the defense with this arm in an obvious way even though this is a foul. As you get more accustomed to contact, you will use the nondribbling arm in a more subtle manner.

5. Repeat this twice. Then repeat again, switching dribbling hands every 5 seconds.

Protecting the Ball
while Dribbling

non ball arm
is out, not
tucked in

6. Repeat again, allowing an assistant walking around to hand signal the change in dribbling hand. This is most difficult as well as beneficial.

Key Points

1. The defense goes after the ball aggressively causing body contact. A lazy defense makes this lesson of less worth. The defense continuously moves around, not through, the offense for the ball.

2. Players can foul each other for a week at most. If the defense is a non-player, more contact is okay.

3. Keep your head up while you are dribbling. Dribbling with the head down is a waste of time.

4. Use your body and arm to protect the ball.

5. Keep the ball low to the ground.

6. No running away from the defense. Only swivelling allowed.

More Expert Lessons

Protect with 2 on D

Repeat this lesson with two players on defense (if you dare). Always keep your back on one of the players and your arm on the other. In a sense you will always have one player boxed out. An assistant walking around can hand signal for a pass to make this lesson even more beneficial.

Dribbler vs Dribbler

Each dribbler aggressively goes after the ball of the other while protecting their own dribble. Again, no running away, stay in a small area like the lane. Move around each other with heads up. Contact is okay. Avoid obvious fouls.

6 Dribble with D Layup

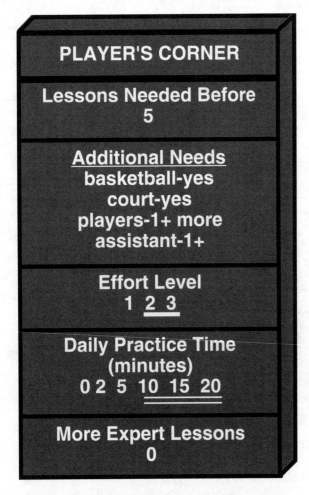

PLAYER'S CORNER

Lessons Needed Before
5

Additional Needs
basketball-yes
court-yes
players-1+ more
assistant-1+

Effort Level
1 <u>2</u> 3

Daily Practice Time
(minutes)
0 2 5 <u>10 15 20</u>

More Expert Lessons
0

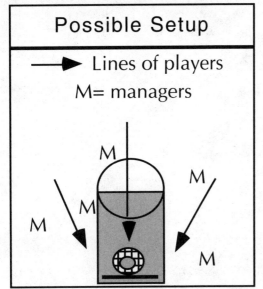

Possible Setup

→ Lines of players

M= managers

Brief:

Assistants as well as other players go for the ball of a player dribbling back to and from a layup line.

Why Do This

This lesson provides game type dribbling practice. In a game the dribbler must look in all directions, even behind, to protect the ball. In this lesson you dribble in a crowd around the basket. After this, dribbling in a crowd in a game is easy by comparison. Players improve quickly.

To gather the large number of assistants and players needed to go after the ball as you dribble, try this. Join a group of players shooting at a basket. Make sure they are friends or at least friendly. Ask all of them to go after the ball for a second or two. If needed stir up lazy friends by knocking away or stealing their ball. Chances are they will readily reciprocate.

Directions

1. Assemble a group of players to go after the ball. Dribble to one of the layup positions–left, right, or center–protecting the ball. Shoot, rebound, and then dribble to one of the other layup lines.

2. Assistants and other players go for the ball for only a second or two, while the player is dribbling.

3. To assistants–go after every ball nearby. Be tricky in your efforts to knock the ball far (very, very far) away from the dribbler. Look especially for a dribbler contemplating sneaker laces. Don't run after players.

4. Dribblers protect the ball at all times. Run after it if it gets knocked away. Run back as well.

Key Points

1. Nobody chases players around the gym. A 1-2 second effort is enough.

2. Assistants should knock the ball in a direction away from the basket.

3. The dribbler hustles after batted balls and then back to the layup line.

4. Protect the ball at all times.

5. Make sure that your head is up, back is nearly vertical, elbows nearly straight. Dribble close to the ground.

6. An easy way to find players to go after the ball is to ask any group shooting the ball at a basket to go after your ball.

7. Initially you can overuse your arm for protection.

7 Dribble Pass with D

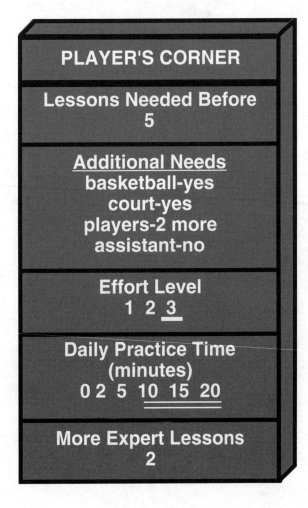

PLAYER'S CORNER

Lessons Needed Before
5

Additional Needs
basketball-yes
court-yes
players-2 more
assistant-no

Effort Level
1 2 **3**

Daily Practice Time
(minutes)
0 2 5 **10 15 20**

More Expert Lessons
2

Brief:
While dribbling downcourt covered by defense, the dribbler passes to a cutter at the basket.

Why Do This

This game level lesson involves many skills. Related lessons are in parenthesis. The dribbler is covered closely while dribbling downcourt looking to pass. At the correct moment a pass is thrown so that the cutter and the ball meet at the basket. Completing this with proper timing of the pass is difficult.

Directions

1. The cutter starts in either corner. Cut within 5 seconds after the dribbler starts.

2. Starting at midcourt the dribbler moves toward the basket. Pass to the cutter when she/he cuts to the basket and then follow the pass to the basket.

3. Time the pass so that it **meets** the cutter at the basket. The cutter shoots a one foot shot or layup.

4. The defense covers the dribbler. Force left or right. Follow the pass to the basket. If the shot is missed, go for the rebound.

5. Players rotate positions after every 3-5 tries.

Key Points

1. This lesson is difficult because of the many skills involved. It is not for novices.

2. The dribbler must dribble with the head up and eyes on both the defense and down court on the cutter.

3. The pass must meet the cutter at the basket. The cutter should not need to wait or slow down to catch the pass if the timing is right. This is an important part of this lesson.

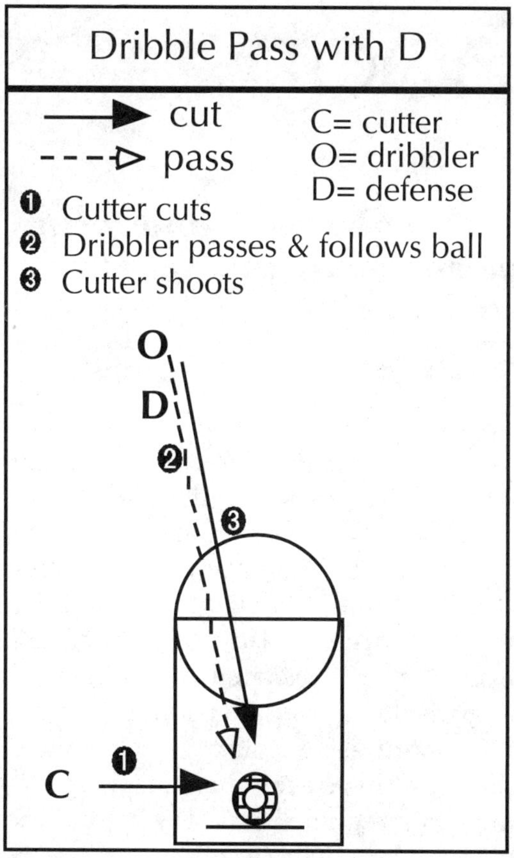

Dribble Pass with D

→ cut
- - -▷ pass

C = cutter
O = dribbler
D = defense

❶ Cutter cuts
❷ Dribbler passes & follows ball
❸ Cutter shoots

4. The passer and defense sprint to the basket after the pass.

More Expert Lessons

Dribbler Shoots It

The cutter in this lesson cuts to the low post, catches the pass, and then gives the ball back to the dribbler for a layup. If the dribbler is not open, the cutter pivots around and shoots. The defense must stay with the dribbler. Passing off and then cutting to the basket, or toward the ball, is called *give and go*. Often the player who first passed the ball is open for a return pass or possible layup.

8 Dribble Full Shoot

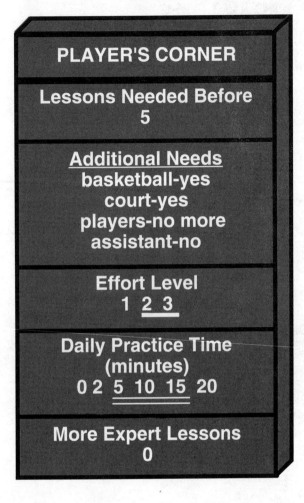

PLAYER'S CORNER

Lessons Needed Before
5

Additional Needs
basketball-yes
court-yes
players-no more
assistant-no

Effort Level
1 <u>2</u> 3

Daily Practice Time (minutes)
0 2 <u>5 10 15</u> 20

More Expert Lessons
0

Brief:

A player dribbles back and forth from one basket to another shooting at each basket.

Why Do This

This is a shooting lesson that involves more dribbling than shooting, but you can emphasize different aspects and practice both skills. Here is the rationale for the shooting part. In a game players shoot while out of breath after sprinting down court many times. Shots are not taken 10 in a row while you are nice, tidy, and rested. A good game shooter practices in a game-like way. This lesson gives you a way. You run full court shooting one shot at each basket. More time is spent dribbling in this lesson than shooting. Switch hands on a regular basis. Try behind the back between the legs dribbles often.

Directions

1. Run down one end and shoot, get the rebound, run down the other end and shoot. It is optional to follow it up if you miss. Pace yourself. Don't stop moving.

2. Switch the dribbling hand on a regular basis. Trick dribble between the legs and behind the back often. Keep the body and ball low even though there is no defense.

3. Shoot from any distance, any place on the court: foul line, 3 pointers, corners, top of the key, one foot shots.

4. Run for 5-20 minutes.

Key Points

1. This is particularly helpful to experienced players practicing long shots. Novice players work on short shots.

2. Novice players, in particular, need to dribble with the head up and the ball low to the ground. This emphasis creates a dribbling lesson.

3. Keep moving for 5-20 minutes. The longer the better because the more tired you are the more worthwhile the lesson. This simulates your condition in a game.

4. Warm up with another shooting lesson at the technique level before doing this. Work on the wrists, and flick ups and other shooting technique lessons.

9 Driving to the Basket

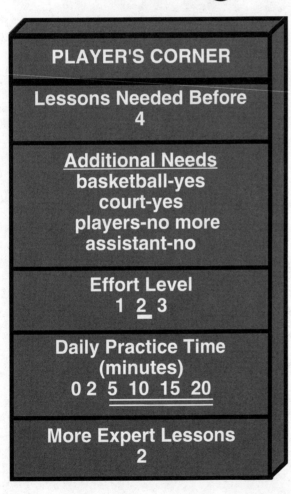

PLAYER'S CORNER

Lessons Needed Before
4

Additional Needs
basketball-yes
court-yes
players-no more
assistant-no

Effort Level
1 <u>2</u> 3

Daily Practice Time
(minutes)
0 2 <u>5 10 15 20</u>

More Expert Lessons
2

Brief:
From the foul line you drive left and right starting with either foot as the pivot.

Why Do This

Players get their steps together for each drive like a hurdler getting steps together between hurdles. Righties always shoot off the left foot and lefties off the right foot. For moments when righties use the left hand they are considered lefties; lefties using the right hand are considered righties. Practice the four possible drives in this order (eight if you practice with both hands):

1. Left foot as pivot and go right.

2. Right foot as pivot and go right.

3. Left foot as pivot and go left.

4. Right foot as pivot and go left.

Do these at a moderate pace; no need to go quickly. Slow down if you encounter difficulty or feel awkward.

Directions

1. Start from a half down position with the ball at waist height.

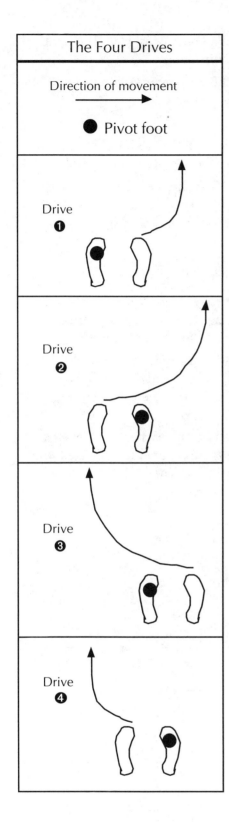

The Four Drives

Direction of movement

● Pivot foot

Drive ❶

Drive ❷

Drive ❸

Drive ❹

2. Push the ball low, far to the side of the drive.

3. The first step is a long one, so that you get past the defense.

4. You must step around the defense, not through them, so move slightly sideways before moving forward. Use a chair or another person as dummy defense to step around.

5. Dribble the ball as you take the first step.

6. Do not drag the pivot foot.

7. Right handers always shoot off the left foot on either side of the basket and left handers always off the right foot.

8. Novice players take as many steps and dribbles as necessary to complete the move, whereas experienced, taller players can limit the steps to between 2 and 4.

9. Use only 1 or 2 dribbles. Do each drive 10 times if it feels uncomfortable, five otherwise.

10. Experienced players repeat this lesson with the opposite hand.

Key Points

1. Have someone watch you for dragging the pivot foot and stepping before dribbling..

2. Use a chair or another person as a defensive player to drive around. Step around the defense on the first step. When past the defense, reach around and out with the inside elbow to keep the defense behind.

3. Practice slowly. Speed naturally increases with repetition. You need to feel comfortable while practicing.

4. Always shoot off the left foot when shooting with the right hand and off the right foot when shooting with the left hand.

5. Push the ball far to the side of the drive low to the ground.

More Expert Lessons

Fake Then Drive

Players often fake before driving. Execute the fake slowly so the defense has time to react. The defense can't react to a quick fake. Two types of fakes are used. Do each drive 5-10 times.

1. A step fake is used before the crossover step in drive 2 and 3 above. (a. Right foot as pivot and go right. b. Left foot as pivot and go left.)

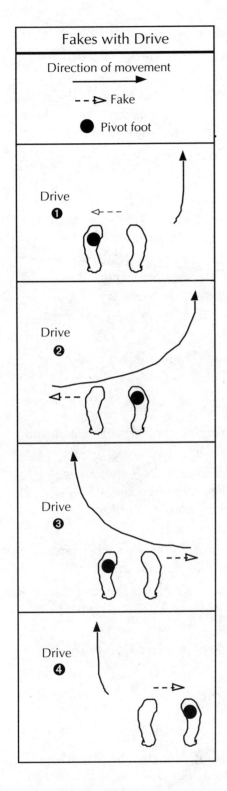

Fakes with Drive

Direction of movement

- - ▷ Fake

● Pivot foot

Drive ❶

Drive ❷

Drive ❸

Drive ❹

2. Slowly push the ball and the body away from the pivot foot as you step in that same direction.

3. Bring the ball back, take the crossover step more quickly, and drive to the basket.

4. Do each drive 5 times.

5. Use a ball body fake for drives 1 and 4 above. (**a.** Left foot as pivot and go right. **b.** Right foot as pivot and go left.)

6. Push the ball and slightly turn the body in the opposite direction of the drive.

7. Then take a step and move the ball low to the outside direction of the drive.

Drive Opposite Foot

•This is only for experienced players for two reasons. One, this lesson undoes the fundamentals you are learning. Two, this move is only needed to beat very tall players.

•This layup is taken off the wrong foot on purpose. The advantage is that the defense is not ready for it. They expect you to take one and a half steps before shooting. This is especially effective against big players.

•Do this opposite foot drive using the same four moves as in the more regular drives. The layup is usually released one step farther from the basket than normal.

10 Take Away

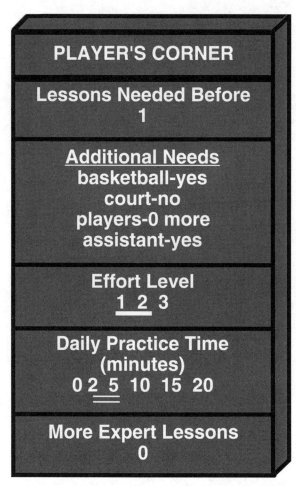

Brief:

An assistant or player holds the ball at various heights while the other player grabs and then pulls the ball away.

Why Do This

Grabbing is a precursor to both catching and rebounding. Do this lesson slowly at first.

Directions

1. An assistant tightly holds the ball at waist height with the ends of the fingertips.

2. Grab the ball with the fingertips and rip it 2-4 feet away. Repeat this at least 3-5 times.

3. The assistant next holds the ball low, or you can place the ball on the floor. Stretch low for the ball, grab and pull it away. Repeat 3-5 times.

4. The assistant next holds the ball high, or you can toss it one foot overhead. Reach high, grab, and pull the ball away.

5. The assistant holds the ball high enough overhead to make you jump for it.

Take Away Setup

hold out ball

grab and pull away

Key Points

1. Emphasize that the ball needs to be both held and grabbed using the finger ends. Overdo it. Palms do not touch the ball.

2. Pull the ball away with much effort. This is similar to grabbing a rebound or stealing the ball.

3. Players tend to underdo all technique level lessons. Watch closely and (over) emphasize overdoing it.

4. Players both pull the ball and turn away at the same time.

Hold High

Hold Low

11 Move Ball

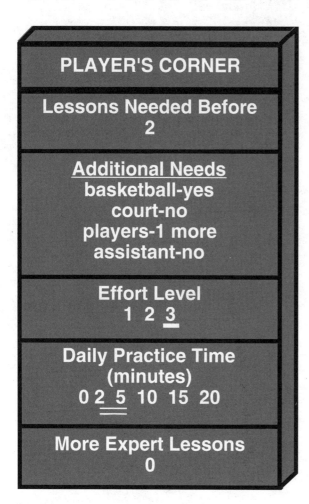

PLAYER'S CORNER

Lessons Needed Before
2

Additional Needs
basketball-yes
court-no
players-1 more
assistant-no

Effort Level
1 2 <u>3</u>

Daily Practice Time
(minutes)
0 2 <u>5</u> 10 15 20

More Expert Lessons
0

Brief:

One player quickly moves a ball right in front of another who attempts to take it away.

Why Do This

Closely covered offensive players must move the ball quickly to avoid getting tied up. This type of ball movement is also used in other moves. The defense learns how to tie up the offense without fouling. Young players, in particular, often flail their arms and hands at the ball when going for it. Fouls are called not only when there is actual contact, but also when it looks like contact. This lesson helps to prevent both many unnecessary fouls and players from fouling out.

Directions

1. Two players, 2 feet apart, face each other. The player with the ball does not move his or her feet once set.

2. The defense goes after the ball without fouling. Flailing the arms without contact is also considered a foul. If you foul in this way or by contact, you stay on defense. The defense loudly counts to 10 and then stops.

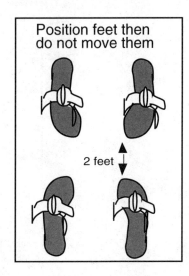

Position feet then do not move them

2 feet

3. The offense moves the ball quickly, keeping it away from the defense. You can bend your knees, rotate your hips, and move the ball high to low, left to right and near to far from the body. Call out contact fouls.

4. The defense can move their feet more as the offense becomes more adept at moving the ball.

Key Points

1. The objective is to move the ball, not the body. Keep both feet in place.

2. The offense calls contact fouls. Flailing is a foul even if there is no contact.

3. Offensive players tend to move their feet and body to protect the ball. Keep the ball out in front during this lesson.

4. Young defensive players too readily foul the offense. This is why the offense must loudly call fouls.

Move the Ball

high to low

left to right

near to far

12 Grab Full Court

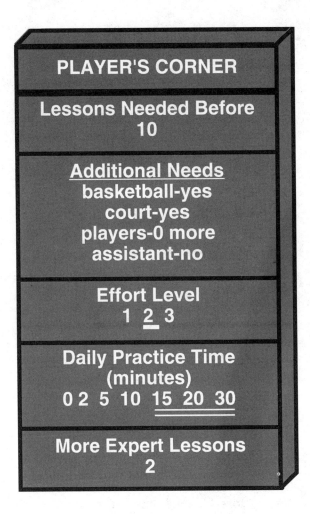

PLAYER'S CORNER

Lessons Needed Before
10

Additional Needs
basketball-yes
court-yes
players-0 more
assistant-no

Effort Level
1 <u>2</u> 3

Daily Practice Time
(minutes)
0 2 5 10 <u>15 20 30</u>

More Expert Lessons
2

Brief:
Two players run a full court circuit while executing the grabbing lesson.

Why Do This

This is a continuous motion lesson. While practicing the ball handling skills, you move continuously for the allotted amount of time around a circuit between the two baskets. The movements in this lesson may look funny, but it is of great value. Besides practicing the ball handling skills and becoming more conditioned, players shoot a layup at each basket. Players also need to communicate as they move between each basket. More coordination is needed to grab the ball while running than when stationary. Run at a comfortable pace. If you are out of shape go slower. Players tend to go too fast at first.

Directions

1. This is a continuous movement lesson, and it means just that, no stopping. Move for 15 minutes initially and add to this each day. You do not need to run at top speed; pace yourself so that you can finish. If you are out of shape,

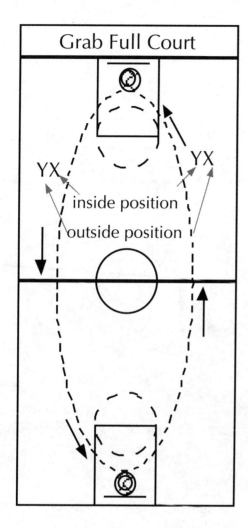

Grab Full Court

YX — inside position
— outside position
YX

force yourself to go slow. As you run the circuit, grab the ball back and forth as you did in the previous lesson.

2. Run down the right side of the court. Shoot a layup at the basket. Then run down the other side of the court to the other basket. Players alternate shooting the layup.

3. At no time does the ball bounce on the ground.

4. Change direction every few minutes. Stop, turn around and go in the opposite direction.

5. Also switch inside and outside positions also after each basket.

6. Change grabbing position each minute. Start out holding the ball at waist level. *Grab high* means to hold the ball over your head. *Grab low* means to gently roll the ball on the ground ahead of the other player. See the extensions below to add more variety to this lesson.

Key Points

1. The ball never bounces on the floor—while grabbing, before shooting, or on the rebound. No dribbling.

2. Keep your heads up so that you do not run into other players on the court.

3. Stop or slow down before taking the layup.

4. Make your partner reach and then grab for the ball.

5. There will be mismatches in terms of conditioning. Find someone approximately in the same condition to work with.

6. After each basket, switch inside-outside positions.

More Expert Lessons

Short Pass Full Court

There are many types of short passes that can be practiced in the continuous motion lesson. All of these improve not only the particular pass, but also all ball handling skills.

1. The **hand off** is actually not a pass. One player gives it to the other.

2. The **lateral** is a short pass. It is thrown under handed.

3. The **overhead hook** pass is also practiced with each hand.

•Players need to stay close for passes numbered 3 to 5.

4. The **behind the back** pass needs to be practiced with each hand.

Short Passes

hand off

lateral

hook

behind back

bounce

5. The **bounce** pass is the exception to the no bounce rule.

Tricky Pass Full Court

Do these near the end of the lesson. You will have difficulty and some fun. If you lose the ball, speed up to recover it.

1. The **between the legs** pass is a lateral type pass. Do it with each hand.

2. The **bounce between the legs** pass is another easier one that can be done. Do it with each hand as well.

3. Invent a pass by combining two types of passes. For example, players can move the ball around their back, then throw a hook or lateral pass.

4. Another combination—move the ball between the legs; no bouncing; then use a bounce pass. Their are many combinations to try. Don't worry about walking in this lesson.

5. With more experienced players, one player can harass the shooter.

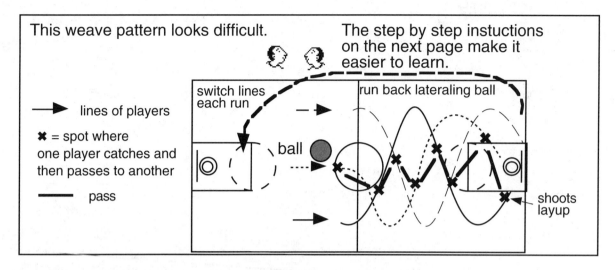

This weave pattern looks difficult.

The step by step instuctions on the next page make it easier to learn.

→ lines of players

✖ = spot where one player catches and then passes to another

—— pass

switch lines each run

ball

run back lateraling ball

shoots layup

13 Front Weave

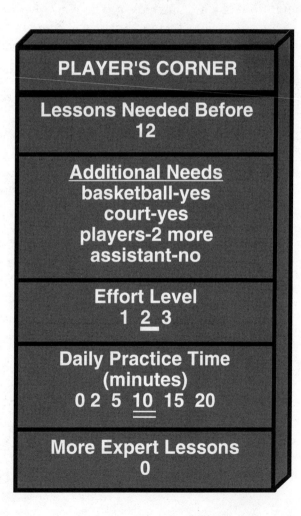

PLAYER'S CORNER

Lessons Needed Before
12

Additional Needs
basketball-yes
court-yes
players-2 more
assistant-no

Effort Level
1 2 3

Daily Practice Time
(minutes)
0 2 5 10 15 20

More Expert Lessons
0

Brief:

Three players weave the ball from midcourt to the basket.

Why Do This

This super lesson improves passing, cutting, and especially timing skills. Players enjoy it and also get a great workout. Novices may need several days to learn the weave pattern. This lesson is much easier if performed with 2 players. So you may want to try it this way if there is a problem.

Directions

1. Players start at midcourt in 3 lines. The one in the center has the ball; the others are 5 yards to either side.

2. Each player runs a zigzag pattern across the court from the left to the right and back again until the basket is reached. The player with the ball at the basket shoots the layup. Let's walk through it first. (See the diagrams.)

3. Start the weave with the ball in the center. These directions mostly detail the movements of the player starting in the central position.

4. The player on the right cuts 3 yards in front of the player with the ball to receive a pass.

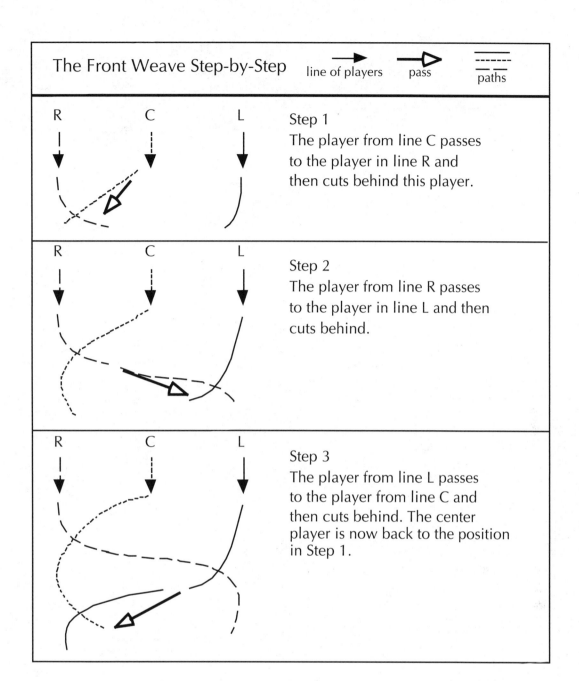

The Front Weave Step-by-Step   line of players   pass   paths

Step 1
The player from line C passes to the player in line R and then cuts behind this player.

Step 2
The player from line R passes to the player in line L and then cuts behind.

Step 3
The player from line L passes to the player from line C and then cuts behind. The center player is now back to the position in Step 1.

Catch the ball slightly to your side of center. Take 2 to 3 steps after catching the ball before passing to the player 3 yards ahead of you–the starting left side player.

5. After passing, the starting center player continues to move diagonally toward the sideline. When you go about 5 yards to the right, turn and cut toward the center again.

6. Cut in front of the left side player who now has the ball. You should receive a pass slightly left of center. Take a step or two and pass ahead to the player cutting in front. Continue moving toward the sidelines. Five yards to the left, turn and head diagonally down court.

7. Continue this zigzag pattern until you reach the basket.

8. If a bad pass is thrown, continue running. The player closest to the ball sprints after it and then passes to a teammate who is probably near the basket by this time.

9. When players are more expert, direct them to use bounce passes.

Key Points

1. It is a good idea to watch experienced players do this at full speed.

2. Walk through this initially.

3. Players run 3-5 yards toward the sidelines after the pass and then turn and cut to the center for the ball.

4. If you are next to receive a pass, always cut diagonally in front of the player with the ball.

5. Once you have passed the ball, always cut behind the player with the ball.

6. Don't worry about *walking* initially.

7. Inform novices that this may take several days to learn so they will not be disappointed.

14 Back Weave

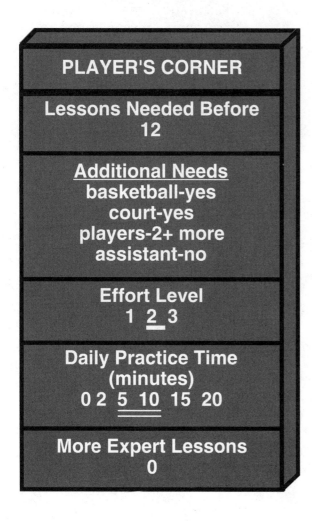

PLAYER'S CORNER
Lessons Needed Before **12**
Additional Needs **basketball-yes** **court-yes** **players-2+ more** **assistant-no**
Effort Level 1 <u>**2**</u> 3
Daily Practice Time **(minutes)** 0 2 <u>**5 10**</u> 15 20
More Expert Lessons **0**

Brief:

Players weave the ball back and forth between two lines.

Why Do This

This is a safe way to hand off the ball if the defense is playing a tight person-to-person defense. Players without the ball cut behind (away from the basket) the player with the ball. Both before and after lateraling, the passer picks the defense on the catcher. This lesson is usually for more experienced players.

Directions

1. One player starts on each side of the court 5 yards up court from the corner. A player with the ball stands at the top of the key facing the direction of the cutter, which initially is the left sideline.

2. A cutter from the left side runs directly toward the ball. When 1-3 feet away, grab the lateral and move slightly toward midcourt avoiding a collision with the passer. It is okay to bump into or rub shoulders with the passer.

3. The player giving up the ball pivots to block the path of the defensive player on the catcher. Be careful not to step into the defense. You

The Back Weave Step-by-Step	
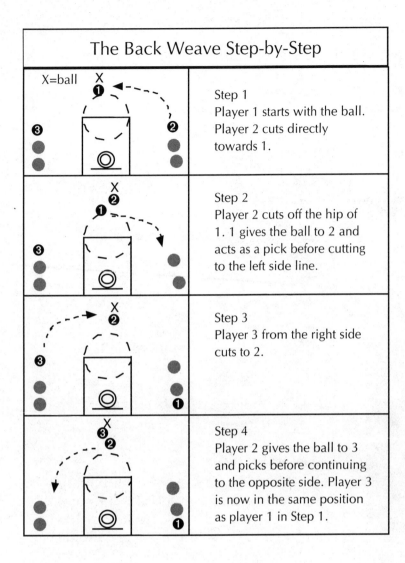	**Step 1** Player 1 starts with the ball. Player 2 cuts directly towards 1.
	Step 2 Player 2 cuts off the hip of 1. 1 gives the ball to 2 and acts as a pick before cutting to the left side line.
	Step 3 Player 3 from the right side cuts to 2.
	Step 4 Player 2 gives the ball to 3 and picks before continuing to the opposite side. Player 3 is now in the same position as player 1 in Step 1.

want this defensive player to *wipe off on you* or step away from the ball. You are a pick with the ball.

4. After giving up the ball, hesitate for 2 seconds as a pick, then go to the left side position.

5. A player from the opposite side, now the right side, cuts to the ball and the weaving is continued.

6. To keep the weave moving, cut to the ball just before the previous lateral is made.

Key Points

1. The passer laterals and acts like a pick.

2. The passer faces the direction of the cutter and pivots around and laterals at the same time.

3. The cutter cuts directly to the ball (and the passer) and actually rubs shoulders with the passer on (or slightly after) the lateral.

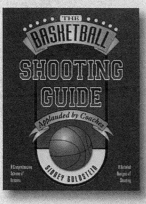
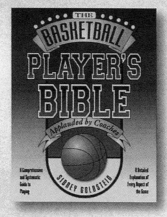

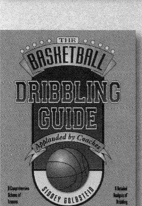

about The Basketball Coach's Bible

The Basketball Coach's Bible is aptly described by knowledgeable coaches as "long overdue" and "more detailed" than any other book on the fundamentals. The author who has successfully coached both men's and women's teams spent three years writing this practical action book so that anyone can coach.

• Part I discusses and graphically defines the fundamentals.

• Part II explains how to plan–the key to coaching–and teach at practice.

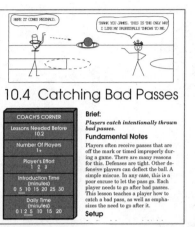

Some diagrams from Lesson 6.5 Hook Shot

Section 12 Defense
Part of S

Number	Lesson	Players	Ball
12.0	**Defensive Position**	1	-
12.1	Move in D Position	1	-
12.2	Force Left & Right1-5	2	-
12.21	Three Yard Lesson	2	-
12.22	Mirror Lesson	2	x
12.3	Trapping 1-3	3	-
12.31	Trapping Game	3	-
12.4	Front Keep Out of Lane	2	x

10.4 Catching Bad Passes

• Part III, the largest part, systematically presents over 200 lessons in 19 sections.

• Twenty-three pages of Appendices supply other useful coaching information such as: strategies; a practice warm down; game statistics and more. The large Index, Table of Contents, and over 400 illustrations help separate this book from lesser efforts.

• This book supplies the know how to teach successfully all players, women and men, of all abilities from Biddy League to professional. With these methods players improved conspicuously during each and every practice. Others can now benefit as well.

To order call 215 438-4459 in Philadelphia or 800 979-8642 nationwide.

The Nitty-Gritty Basketball Series	Description	Cost	#	Total
ISBN 1-884357-01-6 **All 8.5 x 11**	Applauded by coaches as providing the most detailed and understandable explanation of the fundamentals of basketball.	$93.55		
The Basketball Coach's Bible ISBN 1-884357-07-5 350 pages	Everything you need to know about the fundamentals of both coaching and basketball. over 400 illustrations	$24.95		
The Basketball Player's Bible ISBN 1-884357-13-X 270 pages	Everything you need to know about fundamentals and teaching the skills to one or two players. over 300 illustrations	$19.95		
The Basketball Shooting Guide ISBN 1-884357-14-8 45 pages	Teaches shooting techniques that yield rapid and permanent improvement. No more slumps. From *The Basketball Player's Bible.*	$6.95		
The Basketball Scoring Guide ISBN 1-884357-15-6 47 pages	Teaches the moves used by the pros step-by-step. From *The Basketball Player's Bible.*	$6.95		
The Basketball Dribbling Guide ISBN 1-884357-16-4 46 pages	Anyone can be a good dribbler. These methods show how. From *The Basketball Player's Bible.*	$6.95		
The Basketball Defense Guide ISBN 1-884357-17-2 46 pages	Teaches how to play defense in every situation. From *The Basketball Player's Bible.*	$6.95		
The Basketball Pass Cut Catch Guide ISBN 1-884357-18-0 47 pages	The key to being an effective team and all-around player involves these skills. From *The Basketball Player's Bible.*	$6.95		
Basketball Fundamentals ISBN 1-884357-08-3 46 pages	All about the fundamental skills of basketball. From *The Basketball Coach's Bible.*	$6.95		
Planning Basketball Practice ISBN 1-884357-09-1 46 pages	How to plan practice, use time efficiently, keep statistics, use managers, deal with players, and more. From *The Basketball Coach's Bible.*	$6.95		

Shipping charges: $4 1st book, $.50 each add'l bk, $.25 each add'l booklet; booklets only $2 first, $.25 each add'l _____

Up to 50% Off– call for details

PA only–add 6% tax; **Philadelphia** only–add 1% tax _____

Total _____

Satisfaction gauranteed. **To order** send this form with a check to **Golden Aura Publishing, P.O. Box 41012, Phila. PA, 19127**

NAME_____ ADDRESS_____ PHONE _____

CITY_____ STATE_____ ZIP_____ Call for volume **discounts** and special promotions .